Great Empires

The Indian Empire

ELLIS ROXBURGH

WAYLAND

WAYLAND

www.waylandbooks.co.uk

Published in paperback in 2017 by Wayland

Copyright © 2015 Brown Bear Books Ltd

Wayland, an imprint of Hachette Children's Group
Part of Hodder & Stoughton
Carmelite House
50 Victoria Embankment
London EC4Y 0DZ
An Hachette UK Company
www.hachette.co.uk
www.hachettechildrens.co.uk

Dewey number: 909'.0971254-dc23
ISBN: 978 1 5263 0070 6
10 9 8 7 6 5 4 3 2 1

Brown Bear Books Ltd
First Floor
9–17 St Albans Place
London
N1 0NX

Editorial Director: Lindsey Lowe
Managing Editor: Tim Cooke
Children's Publisher: Anne O'Daly
Design Manager: Keith Davis
Designer: Melissa Roskell
Picture Manager: Sophie Mortimer
Production Director: Alastair Gourlay

Printed in China

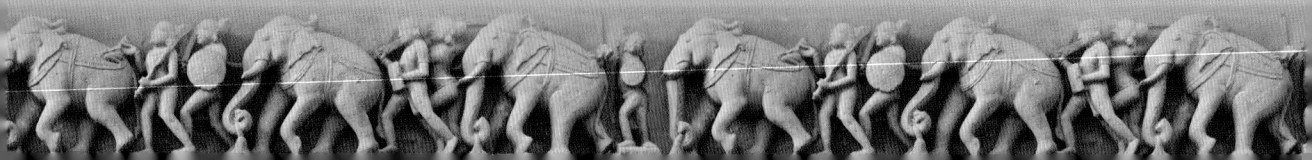

CONTENTS

Introduction

The Mauryan emperors of India once ruled 100 million subjects. Until 100 years ago, however, little was known about their empire.

The Mauryans ruled India over 2,000 years ago, from 322 BCE to about 185 BCE. Great empires have risen and fallen in India since, including the Mughal and the British empires. They came to dominate discussions of Indian history. The Mauryans left few physical traces. Most of their buildings were made from wood, so they have rotted and disappeared. When the last Mauryan emperor was overthrown, the **dynasty** and its remarkable achievements were largely forgotten.

The Great Stupa at Sanchi was one of the most important Buddhist monuments built during the reign of Emperor Ashoka.

A lion sits on top of one of the pillars Ashoka erected throughout the empire. He carved announcements into the stone pillars.

The name of one emperor remained celebrated, however: Ashoka. Ashoka helped to spread Buddhism in Asia. The religion had begun in northern India in the 6th century BCE. After Ashoka came to the throne, he converted to Buddhism. He sent **missionaries** to bring the faith to Thailand, Sri Lanka and other neighbouring states.

For the time, Ashoka was a remarkable ruler. He turned away from war and urged his people to live according to principles of fairness and justice. We know about his

Buddhist monks walk through a village. Ashoka played a key role in the spread of Buddhism in India and elsewhere in Asia.

achievements because he had them recorded in a series of **edicts**, or announcements. These edicts were carved into rocks or on special pillars across the empire. They told Ashoka's subjects how he wanted them to live.

Ashoka was the greatest of the Mauryan emperors. The empire was founded in north-west India by his grandfather, Chandragupta Maurya, in 322 BCE. Chandragupta overthrew Indian states one by one to build an empire that was enlarged by his son, Bindusara. At its greatest extent, the empire covered nearly all of what are now Pakistan and India, and parts of Iran and Afghanistan to the north and west.

Mauryan Empire c. 232 BCE

GANDHARA

● Taxila

KAPILVASTU

MAGADHA ● Pataliputra

SAURASHTRA

Arabian Sea

KALINGA

ANDHRA

Bay of Bengal

CHOLA

Key

Conquests of Chandragupta (322 BCE–298 BCE)

Conquests of Bindusara (298 BCE–272 BCE)

Conquests of Ashoka (c. 268 BCE–232 BCE)

Eastern limit of Macedonian expansion (325 BCE)

INDIAN OCEAN

Ashoka died in 232 BCE. Without the commanding presence of Ashoka, the empire began to break apart. It had become too large to govern efficiently. A series of weak emperors came to the throne. In 185 BCE, less than 50 years after Ashoka's death, the final emperor was assassinated and the Mauryan Empire came to an end.

The Roots of the Empire

During the 4th century BCE, the states of what is now India faced a threat from the West. An outstanding young general was creating a Greek empire that stretched across Central Asia.

In 336 BCE, the young Alexander – later known as Alexander the Great – became king of the Greek kingdom of Macedonia in south-eastern Europe. He led his army through much of the Balkans and West Asia. They defeated all the peoples they met. In 330 BCE, Alexander toppled the mighty Achaemenid Empire of Persia. He burnt the magnificent Persian city of Persepolis. His next target was former Persian territory in what is now north-west India. The campaign lasted two years.

During his campaign across Asia to India, Alexander the Great burnt the renowned Persian city of Persepolis and left it in ruins.

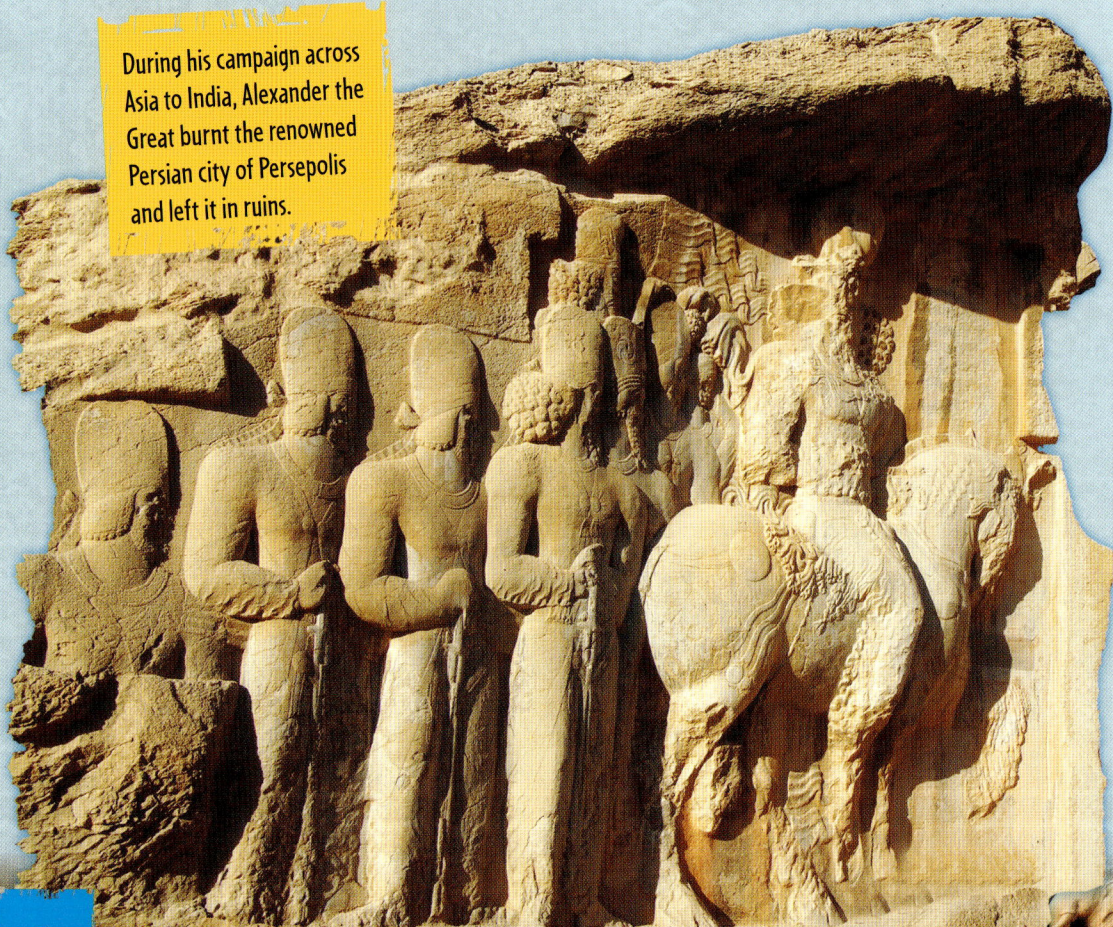

Alexander the Great

Alexander the Great (356 BCE–323 BCE) was educated by the Greek philosopher Aristotle. Alexander inherited the throne of Macedonia after his father was killed. By the age of 25, he had conquered the Persian territories of Asia Minor, Syria and Egypt. Over the next eight years, he created a huge empire that stretched as far as India. Alexander turned back for home in 326 BCE. He died of fever in Babylon a few years later.

This is a statue of Siddartha Gautama, who founded Buddhism in India. By the 4th century BCE, the faith there was in decline.

Alexander Reaches India

By spring 327 BCE, Alexander and his army had almost reached the western bank of the Indus River. Beyond the river, the land that is now Pakistan and India was divided into many small kingdoms. Most of the people followed the ancient Hindu faith, although there were also some Jains and some Buddhists.

News of Alexander's victories and the cruelty with which his army treated their defeated enemies caused panic across the region. Alexander's army captured the province of Gandhara.

Taxila

Taxila, in what is now north-western Pakistan, was the capital of Gandhara. It was wealthy because it stood on three great trade routes. Many rulers wanted to control Taxila, including Alexander the Great. When Alexander arrived in 326 BCE, King Ambhi made a deal to protect his people. The Mauryan Empire later controlled Taxila, but faced frequent revolts against its rule.

The capital of the province was Taxila, between the Indus and Jhelum rivers. King Ambhi of Taxila knew that his people would be slaughtered if they fought, so he did not resist the Greeks. Alexander took Taxila into his empire. The province of Paurava decided to fight. Its army was massacred by Alexander's soldiers.

Alexander Turns Back

Alexander ordered his army to march east into the vast Indian **subcontinent**. His men refused. They wanted to turn back towards home. Alexander was known for his pride and ambition. For reasons that are not fully understood, however, he agreed.

He may have thought that his army was weary. He may also have been worried about the military strength of the neighbouring Magadha Empire.

In July 326 BCE, the Greek army sailed up the Jhelum River on its way home. But it had left a legacy. Many individual Greek soldiers decided to stay behind and settle in north-west India. The Indo-Greek kingdoms they created influenced India for centuries to come.

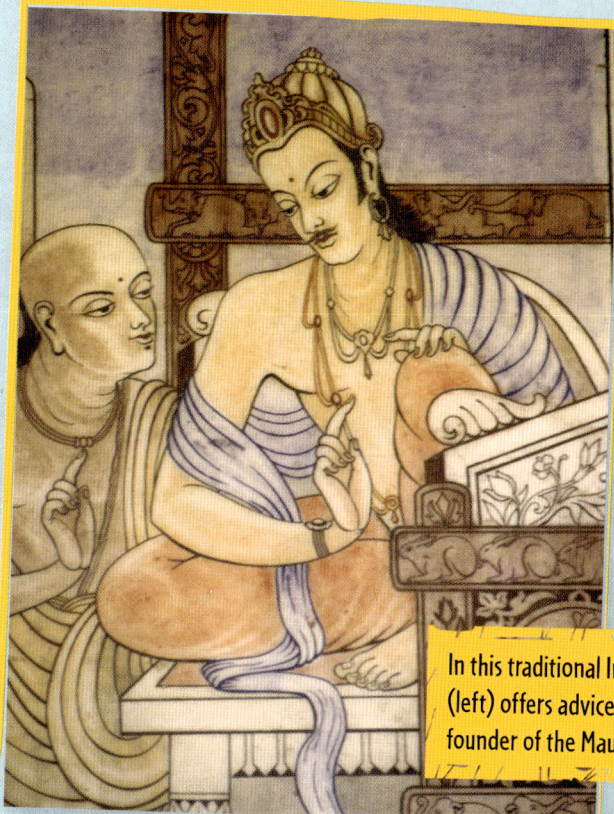

The Magadha Empire

If Alexander had continued into India, he would have encountered the mighty Magadha Empire. Magadha lay south of the Ganges River in what is now the state of Bihar. Magadha was ruled by the Nanda dynasty. The Nandas were known

KEY PEOPLE

Kautilya

Kautilya (370 BCE–283 BCE), also known as Chanakya, was chief adviser to Chandragupta Maurya and his son, Bindusara. Many historians believe Kautilya was the real power behind the Mauryan Empire. He helped Chandragupta to overthrow the Nanda dynasty of Magadha. Kautilya also wrote the *Arthashastra* (see box, page 15). This influential book described how kings should rule their lands. It was thanks to Kautilya that the Mauryan Empire had such an efficient government.

In this traditional Indian painting, Kautilya (left) offers advice to Chandragupta, the founder of the Mauryan Empire.

Religion in India

At the time, the peoples of India followed three main faiths, which all originated on the subcontinent. The oldest and most popular was Hinduism, based on teachings that dated from at least 1700 BCE. Another old faith was Jainism. Chandragupta became a Jain monk after he gave up the Mauryan throne. The third faith, Buddhism, had begun relatively recently. In most of India, however, it was almost unknown at the start of the Mauryan Empire.

for their powerful army. Military strength had allowed Magadha to expand west and south from its heartland east of what is now the city of Varanasi.

Challenging the Nanda

In 321 BCE, this all changed. The ninth Nanda ruler faced a challenge from a young leader named Chandragupta Maurya (340 BCE–298 BCE). Chandragupta did not want to face the Nanda army head on. Instead, he turned to strategy to defeat them. Chandragupta was heavily influenced by a Brahman, or upper-class, adviser named Kautilya, or Chanakya.

Chandragupta and Kautilya had the idea for their strategy after watching a mother feed her son. The woman scolded the boy

The supposed footprints of Chandragupta Maurya were carved into a hill in southern India after he gave up the throne to become a Jain.

Pataliputra stood on the Ganges River. Hindus believed the waters of the Ganges were sacred; they still bathe there today.

for eating from the centre of the dish, which was the hottest part. She told him to eat from the edges, which were cooler. The two men decided to apply the same principle to the Magadha Empire.

The Empire Falls

Chandragupta did not attack the heart of the Magadha Empire. Instead, his men attacked its fringes. They conquered territory little by little until Chandragupta had brought the Ganges Plain under his control. That allowed him to exploit the vacuum left by Alexander's departure from the north-west. Chandragupta captured Magadha and recaptured the provinces that had fallen to the Greeks. He was able to advance rapidly until he reached the Indus River. There he was finally stopped by Alexander's successor, the Greek Seleucus I Nicator. Nicator had fortified the region and defended it well.

Building the Empire

Chandragupta strengthened the empire through warfare and diplomacy. After his death, expansion continued under his son and successor, Bindusara.

Chandragupta Maurya's expansion of his empire was halted by Seleucus I Nicator at the Indus River in 305 BCE. Seleucus had been one of Alexander the Great's generals. He planned to reclaim Alexander's conquests in north-west India. Seleucus had not taken into account the **imperial** ambitions of Chandragupta Maurya, however. When the two armies clashed, the Indian army defeated the Seleucids. The two rulers signed a peace treaty in 303 BCE.

The Rewards of Victory

Under the treaty, Seleucus I Nicator was forced to surrender his lands in what are now present-day eastern Afghanistan, Baluchistan and Makran. He also had to allow his daughter, Cornelia, to marry Chandragupta Maurya. The marriage made a diplomatic union between the new Mauryan Empire and the Hellenistic,

Despite his defeat by the Mauryans, Seleucus I Nicator, shown in this statue, was a successful ruler of the Hellenistic (Greek) Seleucid Empire.

or Greek, world. In return, Chandragupta gave Seleucus 500 war elephants. The Greeks believed these mighty animals were needed for any military victory.

A Military Approach

Chandragupta Maurya now controlled an empire that stretched across the plains of the Indus and Ganges rivers and along the borderlands between Pakistan and Afghanistan. He had gained his territory through warfare. For the rest of his reign, he used the threat of warfare and aggressive diplomacy to reinforce his power. Chandragupta and his adviser, Kautilya, understood that military campaigns were not just about gaining

The Arthashastra

Kautilya, the adviser to the Mauryan emperors, wrote a **treatise** about how kings should rule. *The Arthashastra* discusses economic policy and military strategy. Some historians think Chandragupta Maurya used it as the whole basis for ruling his empire. One of Kautilya's ideas was to use spies to report on what was happening across the empire. The network of spies was a little similar to a modern secret police force.

The Mauryans were famous for their war elephants. They provided the Seleucids with elephants under the terms of the peace treaty.

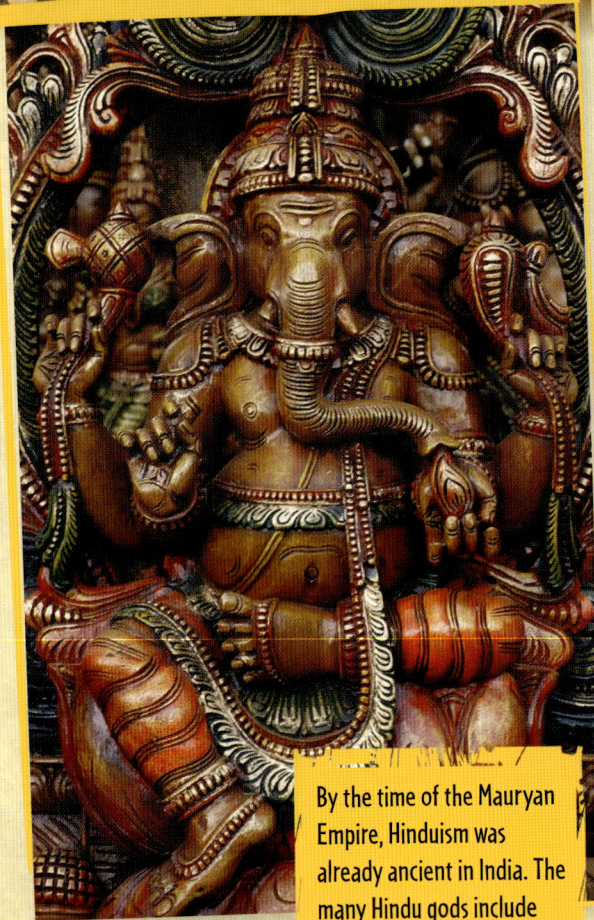

By the time of the Mauryan Empire, Hinduism was already ancient in India. The many Hindu gods include Ganesha, the elephant god.

new territory. With the territory came economic gains. These gains included prisoners of war, who were used as free labour in the expanding empire. The campaign against the Seleucids not only won control of Gandhara. It also gave the Mauryan Empire access to land routes to West Asia.

Chandragupta's Rule

Chandragupta's reign lasted from 322 BCE to 298 BCE. Much of the information we know about him today comes from contemporary accounts written by Greeks. In the accounts, Chandragupta Maurya is known as Sandrokottos. One important record was written by Megasthenes (c. 350 BCE–290 BCE), one of Seleucus's representatives who spent time in the Mauryan

KEY PEOPLE

Sandrokottos

For centuries, historians knew about a Mauryan emperor called Sandrokottos. The Greek Megasthenes wrote about him. It was not until the 18th century, however, that the true identity of Sandrokottos was revealed.

Sir William Jones (1746–1794), a British judge in India and a scholar who could read Greek, Latin, Arabic, Persian and Sanskrit, had a moment of inspiration. He realised that Sandrokottos was Chandragupta Maurya. The discovery allowed historians to go back to other ancient sources to learn more about Chandragupta.

capital, Pataliputra. The presence of Greek diplomats in Pataliputra was to be expected after the marriage between Chandragupta and Seleucus's daughter.

Chandragupta Maurya gave up his throne in 298 BCE in favour of his son, Bindusara (320 BCE–272 BCE). A devoted Jain, Chandragupta spent the rest of his life as an ascetic (holy man). He travelled with other monks to south India. He ended his own life by following the Jain method of slow, controlled starvation.

Bindusara

Bindusara became the second emperor of the Mauryan dynasty. He was known to the Greeks as Amitrochates. Bindusara was just 22 years old

KEY PEOPLE

Megasthenes

Megasthenes was a Greek historian and diplomat. Seleucus I Nicator sent him to Pataliputra, the capital of the Mauryan Empire, during the reign of Chandragupta Maurya. The Greek wrote a four-volume account of India, *Indica*. It was the most complete contemporary account of India as it was in the ancient world.

The influence of the Greeks survived in India for centuries, as in these coins with Greek writing from the 1st century BCE.

Jainism

Chandragupta gave up his throne to follow the principles of Jainism. The Jain religion shares Hindu beliefs in **reincarnation** and **karma**, but Jains do not worship any gods. They live according to three principles called the 'three jewels': right belief, right knowledge and right conduct. They practise **non-violence** towards all living things.

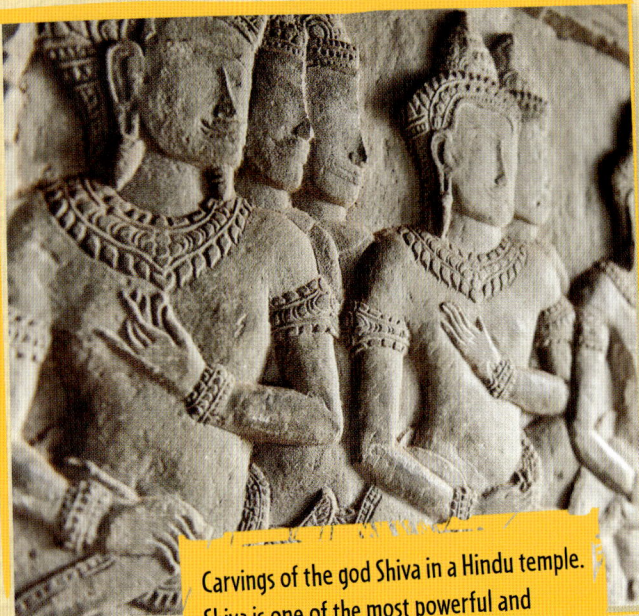

Carvings of the god Shiva in a Hindu temple. Shiva is one of the most powerful and warlike of the many Hindu gods, and is worshipped as the 'destroyer'.

when his father gave up the throne. He inherited an empire from Chandragupta that covered what are now north, central and eastern India. Bindusara expanded the empire southwards into the Deccan Peninsula, as far south as Mysore. The Mauryan Empire included the whole Indian subcontinent apart from Kalinga (modern-day Orissa) and the Tamil kingdoms of the far south.

Bindusara's Reign

Compared with the reigns of his father and his son Ashoka, little is known about Bindusara's reign. One thing that is known is that he continued to use Kautilya as an adviser. Also, the Greeks reported that Bindusara was a man of many interests and tastes. He asked for sweet wine and dried figs from the Greek King Antiochus. Buddhist and Tamil texts describe his military conquests, but he does not seem to have been as aggressive as his father. However, when Bindusara died in 272 BCE, he had brought most of present-day India under his control.

An Heir

Bindusara had many children with many different wives. His chosen heir was his oldest son, Susima (before 304 BCE–

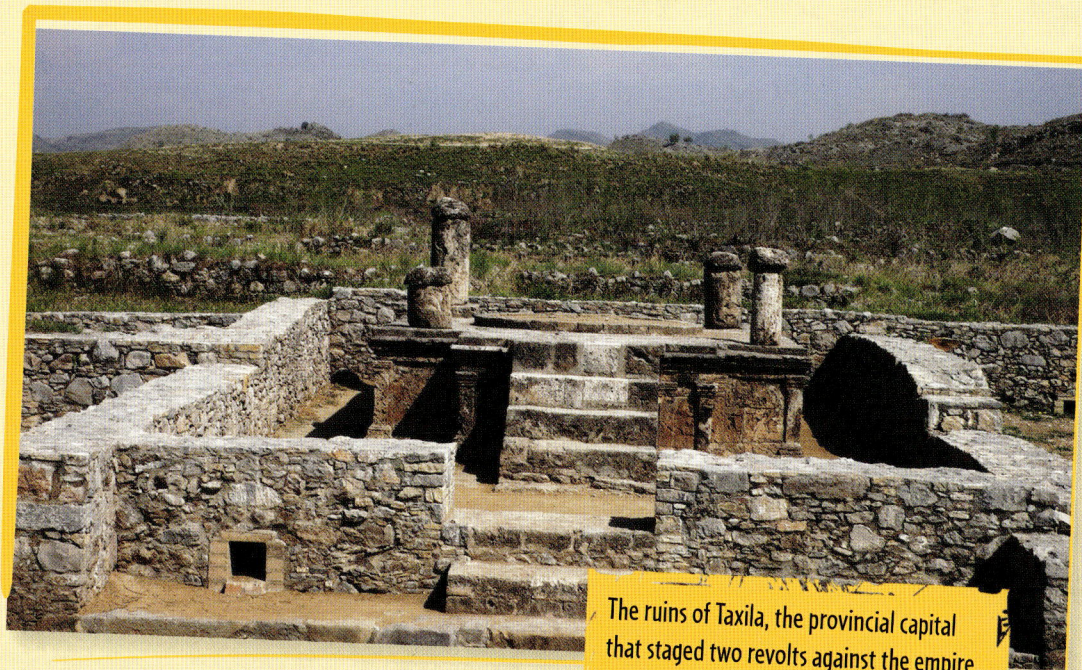

The ruins of Taxila, the provincial capital that staged two revolts against the empire, still stand in what is now Pakistan.

c. 274/270 BCE). To prepare him for his role as emperor, Bindusara sent Susima to Taxila, the capital of Gandhara province, to serve as governor. It seems that Susima's time in Taxila was not a success, however, because there were two known revolts during his governorship. His father, Bindusara, suppressed the first revolt, which was caused by Susima's

KEY PEOPLE

The Birth of Bindusara

According to ancient texts, Kautilya fed tiny amounts of poison to Chandragupta Maurya in his food. This built up the emperor's **immunity** against poisoning by his enemies. The emperor, however, did not know.

One day he fed his pregnant wife some of his food. She had no immunity to poison and died almost immediately. Chandragupta cut open her belly and pulled out the baby. A tiny spot of poison had touched the baby's forehead and turned the skin blue. Chandragupta called his son Bindusara (*bindu* means 'spot' or 'mark' in **Hindi**).

poor government. The cause of the second Taxila revolt is not known, but it was still going at the time of Bindusara's death.

Susima never became emperor. After his father's death, the Mauryan Empire entered a period of civil war. The chief threat to Susima's position came from one of his many half-brothers, Ashoka (304 BCE–232 BCE). Ashoka survived a series of attempts by Susima to **assassinate** him. Instead, Ashoka assassinated Susima sometime between 274 BCE and 270 BCE. Although Bindusara wanted Susima to succeed him, Ashoka had the backing of his father's ministers.

Emperor Ashoka

Ashoka became the third emperor of the Mauryan Empire. He was still young but he was already a fearsome warrior. He had been selected for military training after showing early promise. Some ancient texts claim

This statue shows the Buddha, the Indian teacher whose philosophy of non-violence attracted the emperor Ashoka.

BELIEFS

Hinduism

Ashoka's conversion to Buddhism was unusual because most of his subjects were Hindus. Hinduism began in the Indus Valley in what is now north-west Pakistan.

Hindus believe in an idea called karma, in which every action has a consequence. They also believe in rebirth. There are three main gods – Vishnu, Shiva and Brahma – and thousands of minor gods. Hindus often worship at home, where they make offerings and say prayers.

that he had 99 brothers and that he murdered them all except one. There is no evidence that the story is true. Other stories tell how Ashoka was so strong he killed a lion using just a wooden rod.

Ashoka's reputation as a fearless warrior and tough general led to him being sent to stop riots that had broken out in the Avanti province. Later, he finally put down the riots that his brother Susima had failed to defeat in the city of Taxila.

This Buddhist carving from the 1st century BCE shows a *chakravartin*, or ideal ruler. It may be meant to show Ashoka himself.

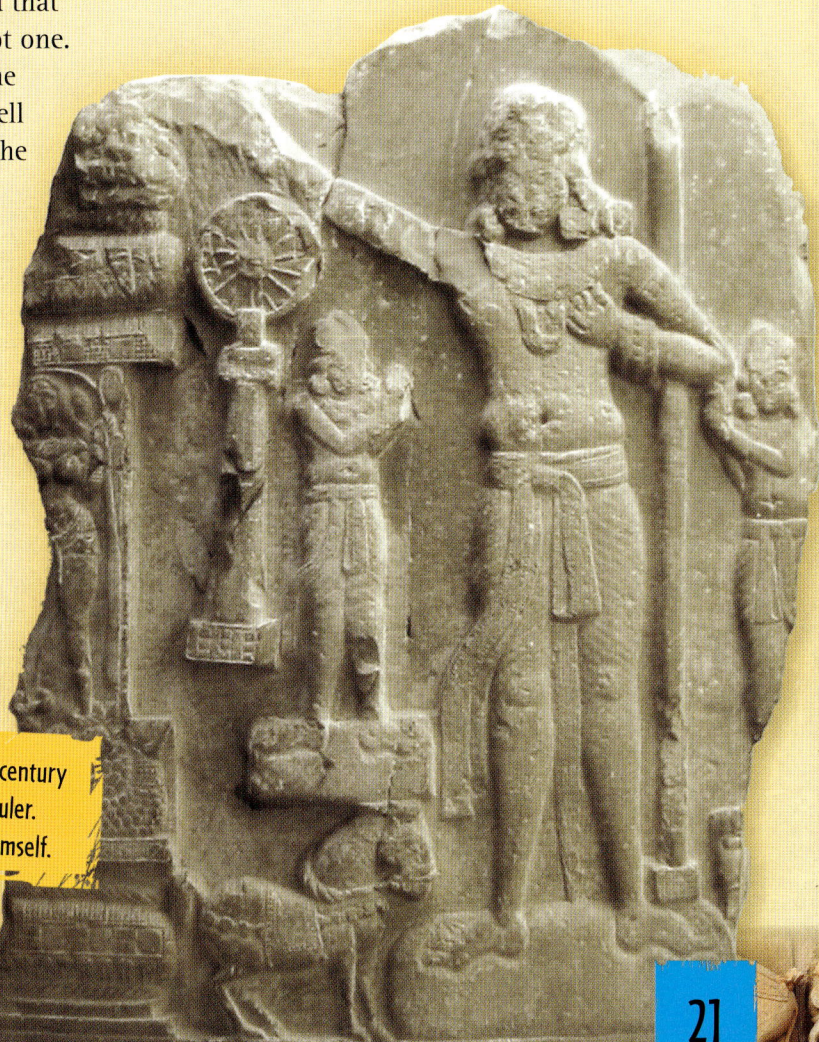

The Height of the Empire

Ashoka was one of the most remarkable leaders in world history. After a dramatic change of beliefs during his youth, he ran his empire based on Buddhist teachings.

Ashoka became emperor in 269 BCE. At the time, the new ruler had a poor reputation. Accounts about his early rule describe a brutal man who did as he pleased. One story says he burnt alive all the women in his palace when they complained he was ugly to look at. He became known as Candasoka, or 'Ashoka the Cruel'. One of his ministers advised him to employ other people to carry out his evil acts. Ashoka took the advice and ordered the building of a prison in which his enemies could be tortured.

Hell on Earth

The prison was beautiful on the outside. Inside, however, it was full of terrible instruments of torture, including some specially invented by Ashoka.

One day, a young Buddhist monk mistakenly came into the prison to ask for **alms**. Instead, he was tortured, but he did

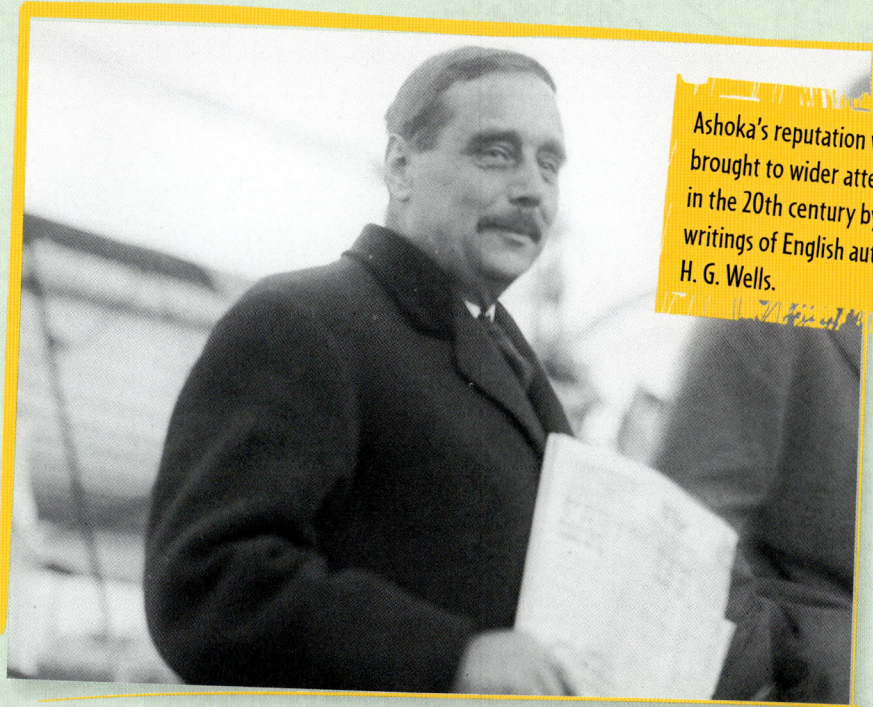

Ashoka's reputation was brought to wider attention in the 20th century by the writings of English author H. G. Wells.

not protest. Some historians believe that Ashoka was so impressed by the monk's behaviour that he decided to **convert** to Buddhism. Others think his conversion was inspired by the Wars of Kalinga.

War in Kalinga

Ashoka fought only one war. Around 260 BCE, he attacked the province of Kalinga (present-day Orissa) on India's east coast. It was the only province to have resisted the expansion of the Mauryan Empire.

The Kalingans were defeated in a brutal war. More than 100,000 men were killed and a further 150,000 deported to work as slaves elsewhere in the empire. Ashoka later had the numbers recorded

KEY PEOPLE

H. G. Wells

The English author H. G. Wells (1866-1946) is famous mainly for science-fiction novels, such as *The War of the Worlds*. But Wells was also responsible for making the Mauryan Empire famous. In 1920 he wrote a best-selling history entitled *Outline of History*. In his chapter on the spread of Buddhism, Wells praised Ashoka's visionary rule. From then on, more people in the West became interested in Ashoka's achievements.

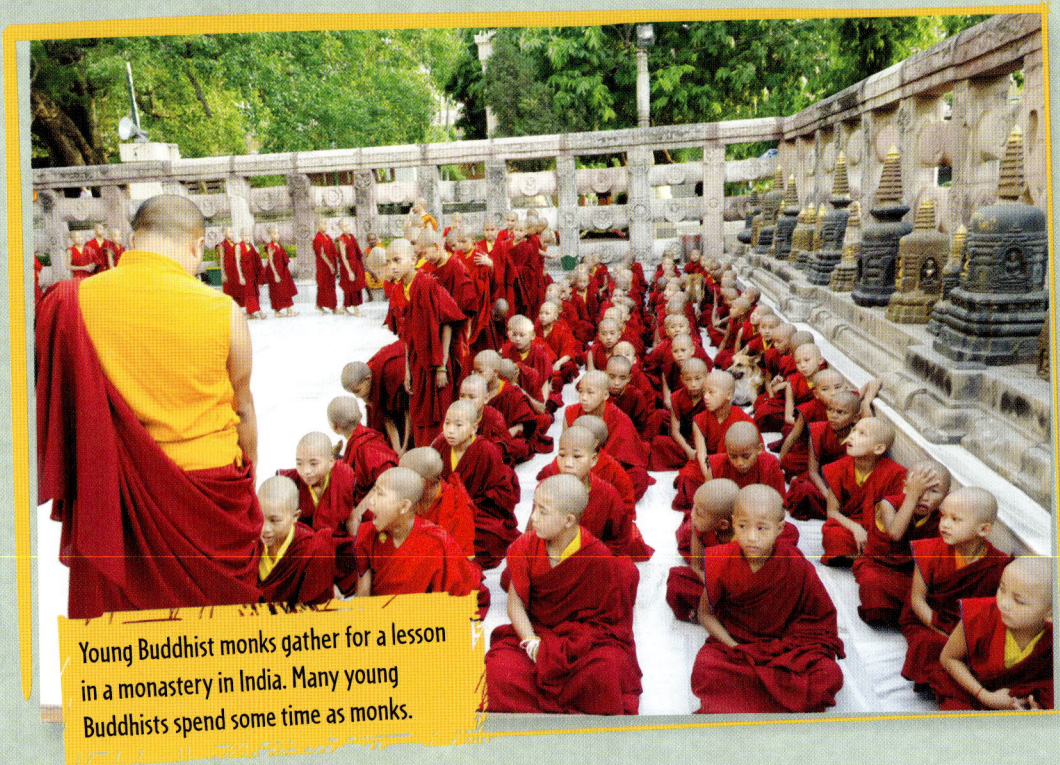

Young Buddhist monks gather for a lesson in a monastery in India. Many young Buddhists spend some time as monks.

BELIEFS

Buddhism

At the time of Ashoka's rule, Buddhism was 400 years old. The religion was founded by an Indian prince who became a monk named Buddha, or 'The Awakened One'. Buddhism has no gods. It teaches that nothing is permanent and that people should aim to reach Enlightenment. This is a state that brings an end to life's suffering.

in an edict, or announcement, carved into a piece of rock. The edict said that Ashoka had visited the battlefields. He was so horrified by what he saw that he decided it was too high a price to pay for victory. He gave up violence and began to explore the teachings of Buddhism. There would be no future conquests through war.

Kautilya, the royal adviser, was shocked by Ashoka's conversion. In his treatise *The Arthashastra*, Kautilya said that one of the key responsibilities of a king was to conquer his enemies through warfare. According to a series of edicts later issued by Ashoka, his conversion to Buddhism

Buddhism in Sri Lanka

According to ancient texts in Sri Lanka, one of the missionaries Ashoka sent to spread Buddhism was his son, Mahinda. Mahinda converted the Sri Lankan ruler, King Devanampiyatissa, to Buddhism. He then built monasteries and monuments, including a centre at Mahavihara. According to the stories, Mahinda's sister Sanghamitta was a nun. She brought to Sri Lanka a sapling from the original Bodhi Tree at Bodh Gaya beneath which Buddha had gained Enlightenment. Sanghamitta planted the tree in the grounds of Mahavihara, where it is said to still grow today.

was not immediate. It had taken place over two years. At the end of that time, Ashoka was convinced non-violence and **tolerance** were the only way to govern.

Ashoka sent Buddhist missionaries across his empire and beyond. The monks visited Kashmir, Sri Lanka and the Seleucid and Ptolemic empires. When missionaries visited Sri Lanka, they took a cutting from the Bodhi Tree in Bodh Gaya. This was the tree under which the Buddha was said to have gained Enlightenment.

Ashoka's Edicts

To teach his subjects about Buddhism, Ashoka ordered a series of edicts to be set up

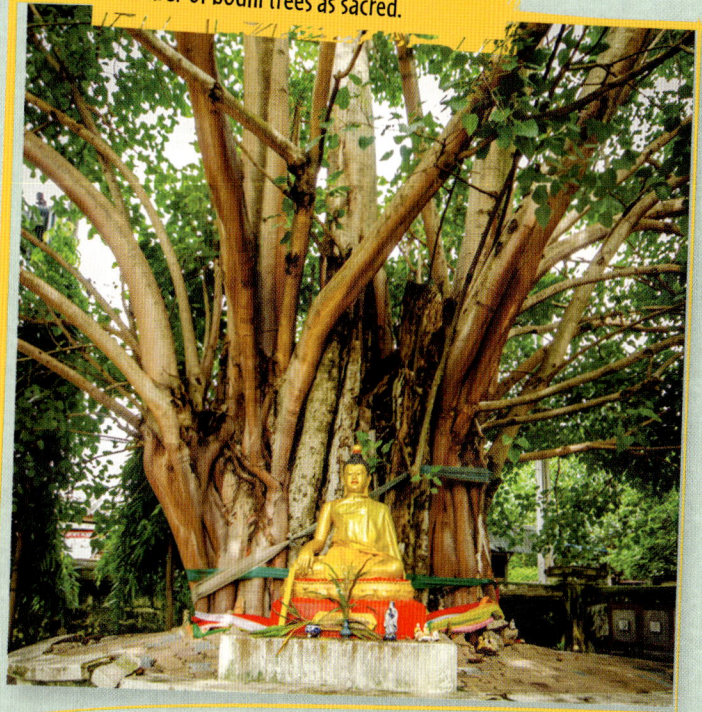

A statue of Buddha sits beneath a huge bodhi tree in India. Today Buddhists see a number of bodhi trees as sacred.

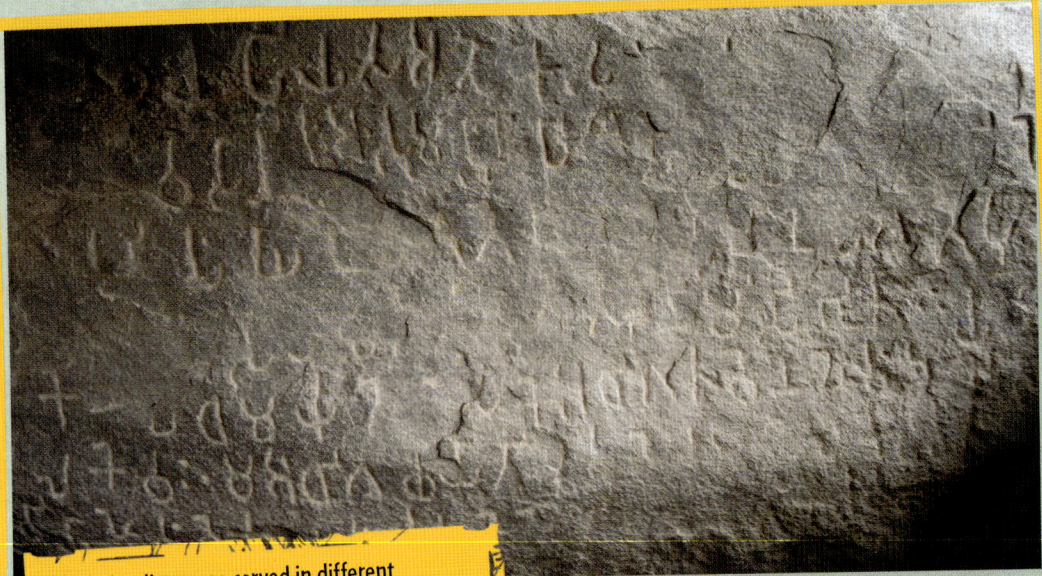

Ashoka's edicts were carved in different languages, including local Indian languages, Greek and Aramaic, a language from the Middle East.

across the empire. There were 26 in all: 14 'major' rock edicts and three 'minor' rock edicts, seven pillar edicts and two minor pillar edicts. The edicts were placed at important points throughout the empire. Their locations show how the empire stretched from present-day Nepal in the north to southern Karnataka in the south, and from Afghanistan in the west and Bangladesh in the east.

The edicts were carved in stone in Prakrit, the local language of Maghada. They were also written in Greek and Aramaic. Although most people were **illiterate**, the edicts were like stone newspapers. Someone who could read would read the edicts out loud, and a crowd would gather to listen. The purpose of the edicts was to

BELIEFS

Dhamma

Ashoka believed in *dhamma*, the Prakrit word for what Buddhists call *dharma*. Ashoka understood *dhamma* to mean a universal law of righteousness. It was a way of living that helped all society and would lead to a more harmonious life. Ashoka wanted to persuade people to live peacefully together without giving in to violence and war.

The Edicts of Ashoka

The Mauryan Empire reached its peak under Ashoka. One way modern historians can tell how big the empire was is the location of Ashoka's edicts. The edicts were announcements that were carved into stone pillars or in large rocks. They were placed across the empire and at its furthest borders. Many edicts survive today. They have been found as far west as Afghanistan and as far south as west-central India.

show Ashoka's people how Buddhism guided his life, especially the principle of *dhamma* (*dharma*). This loosely translates as doing good deeds and treating other people with respect.

Ashoka's Reign

After Ashoka's conversion to Buddhism, he became a kind ruler who was known as Dhammasoka. He set about transforming the lives of his subjects. He ordered wells to be dug to supply fresh water. He also founded hospitals for the sick, and public gardens where medicinal herbs were grown. He recognised that women should be educated and set up schools for girls. He ended discrimination against minorities in the empire. He also tried to provide education for all his subjects, even those belonging to the lowest **caste** in society.

Ashoka's Minor Rock Edict was erected at Guarra in what is now the state of Madhya Pradesh in central India.

The Peoples of the Empire

The Mauryan Empire was based on the defeat of many different kingdoms. The Mauryans allowed some of those kingdoms to keep their powerful rulers and their own armies.

Most of the peoples conquered by the Mauryans were very similar to their rulers. They were Indians descended from the original Aryan inhabitants of the subcontinent. They generally spoke similar languages. The majority of people lived in small villages or towns, where they were farmers or did other jobs on the land. Relatively few of the Mauryans' subjects received much formal education, so they were unable to read. They depended on stories told by professional storytellers or passing travellers for news of what was happening elsewhere.

Regional Differences

There were some differences between the subjects of the empire, however. They were based on geography, religion and caste. Geographically, the north-western part of the empire had once been under the rule of the Greek Achaemenids. There, the Gandharans were known for their skill as musicians, painters and sculptors. They were also fierce warriors. The citizens of the Gandharan capital, Taxila, launched two serious rebellions against Mauryan rule. The edges of the empire,

Ashoka's pillars, like this one next to a Buddhist stupa at Patna, carried his beliefs across the empire.

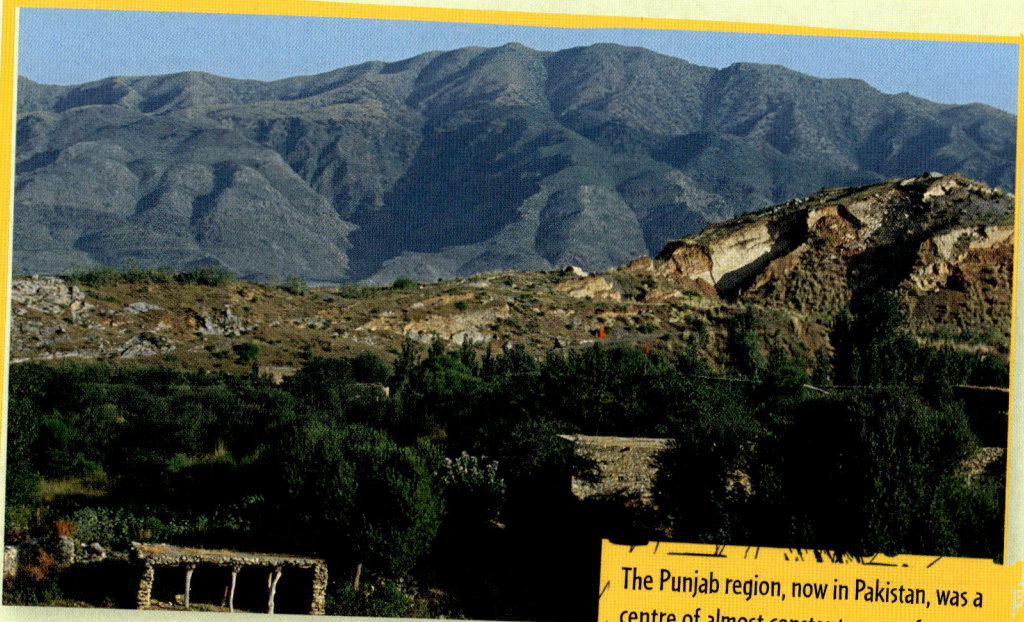

The Punjab region, now in Pakistan, was a centre of almost constant unrest, focussed on the capital, Taxila.

meanwhile, were far less populated. They were home to **nomads**, forest people and hill tribes. The Mauryans mostly left them alone to carry on with their own way of life. These regions were like buffer zones. They protected the empire from its neighbours.

Religious Differences

Another major difference between the subjects of the empire was based on their religion. The vast majority of Indians were Hindus. Their faith was already at least 500 years old in India. Smaller groups of Indians were Jains or Buddhists. Although they were numerically smaller, however, they were highly visible because both

Kalinga

Kalinga (present-day Orissa) was the last region to be absorbed into the Mauryan Empire. With its defeat, all of the Indian subcontinent came under Mauryan control apart from its southernmost tip – Sri Lanka and Kerala were never part of the empire. Kalinga was highly prized because of its rich natural resources, such as rice and wood. Elephants from Kalinga were used as war elephants in the Mauryan army.

Over centuries the Khyber Pass was the main route into India for merchants – and for invading armies.

The Khyber Pass

The Khyber Pass is a key strategic route into the subcontinent. It joins Afghanistan to Pakistan and India. Darius I and Alexander the Great both invaded from the west through the pass. The Mauryans guarded the Khyber Pass against any invasion. They encouraged trade, however. The pass was part of the international trade route known as the Silk Road because silk was one of the goods that passed along it to the West.

religions attracted mendicant, or begging, monks, who were a frequent sight on the empire's roads.

A third source of differences between the Mauryans' subjects was caste. According to Hindu teaching, all Indians were born into one of four social classes, or varnas (see box, opposite page). They stayed in their caste during their entire lives.

A Modern Empire

The Mauryan emperors took an approach towards running their empire that seems quite modern. They understood that their

subjects included many different groups who might be reluctant to change their ways of life. The Mauryans therefore allowed different peoples to continue living as before, but under Mauryan laws.

The empire was divided into four provinces. A prince known as a kumara ruled each province, assisted by a council of officers. One of their chief roles was raising revenue by taxing their subjects. To prevent revolts, the Mauryans had the largest army of the time. It could be quickly sent to any region that rebelled.

The Varnas

According to Hindu teaching, every Hindu is born into one of four castes, which he or she cannot change. The highest caste were Brahmans (priests); next were the Kshatriyas (nobles); third were the Vaisyas (farmers and merchants). The lowest caste were the Sudras (labourers; see box, page 37).

Jain priests in Rajasthan, western India. Although Jainism was a minority religion in India, it was influential in some regions.

Life in the Empire

For most people in the Mauryan Empire, daily life was dominated by the rhythms of farming. Even in the countryside, however, subjects still had to pay taxes to support the empire.

By the time Ashoka became emperor in 269 BCE, the Mauryan Empire was a highly organised state. It had an economy based on agriculture and trade. A period of peace allowed the empire to flourish.

Earlier Indian societies had been mainly urban, but the Mauryans had few large cities. Pataliputra, which Ashoka's grandfather, Chandragupta, had made his capital, remained the most important city.

Up to 100 million people lived in the Mauryan Empire at its height, but most of them lived in small settlements.

The Capital City

Megasthenes, the Greek **diplomat** who wrote about the Mauryans, said that Pataliputra was the largest city in South Asia. He described how the magnificent city stretched for 14 kilometres (9 miles) along the banks of the Ganges River and

Pataliputra stood in a strategic location at the confluence, or meeting, of the Ganges, Son and Gandhaka rivers.

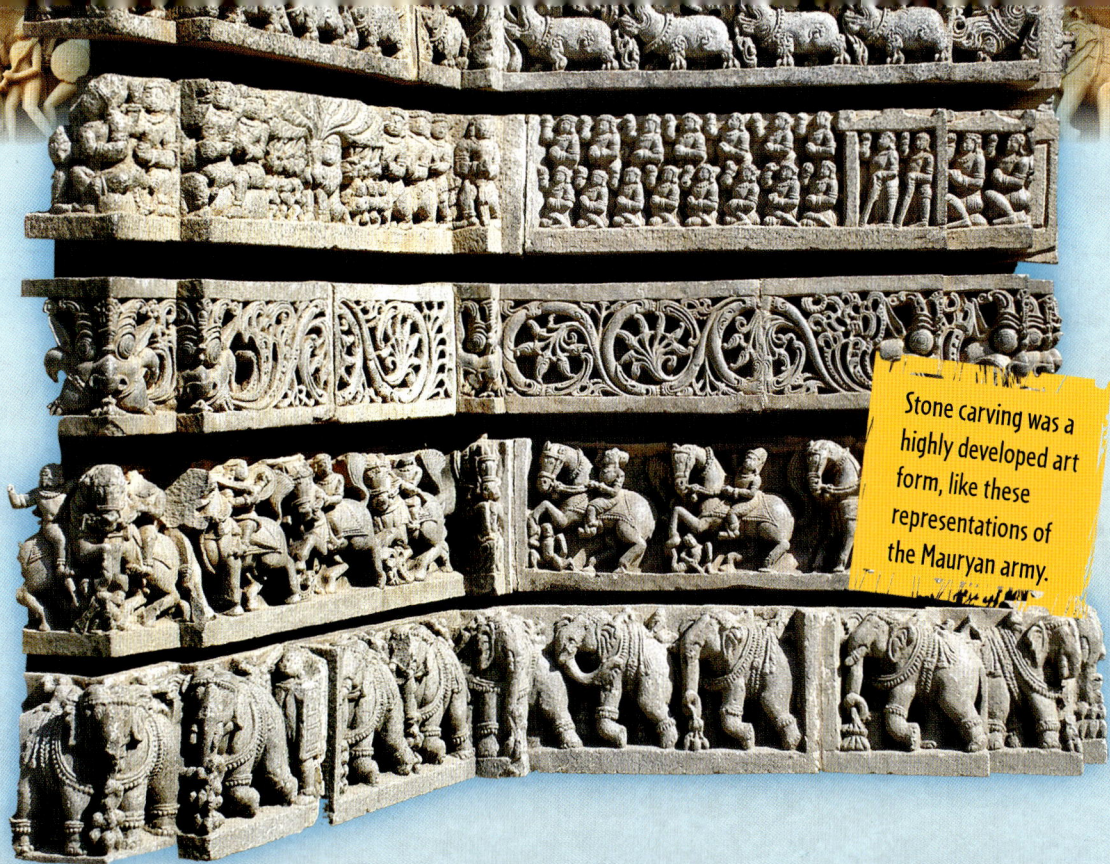

covered around 31 square kilometres (12 square miles). Wooden walls surrounded the city, guarded by 570 watchtowers. Visitors entered and left by one of the 64 city gates. Megasthenes thought Pataliputra was more spectacular than the Persian cities of Susa and Ecbatana, which were famed for their magnificence.

Pataliputra was the only city in the Mauryan Empire with large stone buildings. Historians think that Ashoka replaced the wooden city walls with stone. Elsewhere in the empire, most buildings were made from wood, although a few were made from brick. The wooden structures have rotted over time.

The Capital from Pataliputra

In 1886 archaeologists digging at the ancient site of Pataliputra discovered a stone capital (top of a pillar). It was carved with beautiful rosettes and carved spirals, called volutes. This type of spiral often featured on capitals from Greece. This suggests that Mauryan architecture was influenced by Achaemenid architecture. The capital might even have come from the Thousand Columned Hall said to have once stood in Pataliputra.

Mauryan cities were arranged on a grid system. The royal family or governor lived in a palace. Around the palace, the rest of the city was divided according to the caste system. The Brahman caste lived closest to the palace and the manual workers furthest away. Five boards were responsible for running all aspects of city life, from recording births and deaths to fixing wages and maintaining roads, hospitals, sanitation and educational institutions.

Education

Within the cities, a number of institutions educated people for lives as monks or for government service. Most of the teachers were Brahmans, but Buddhist monasteries were also centres of education. The most

The three-headed lion at the top of one of Ashoka's pillars in the modern city of Mumbai has become a popular symbol of India.

The Mauryan Army

Mauryan soldiers came from all over the empire and from every caste. The army had four branches: chariotry, elephant soldiers, infantry and archers. Archers were the largest branch. At its peak, the army had as many as 750,000 soldiers and more than 9,000 war elephants. Some kingdoms provided soldiers as a form of tax payment.

Today, Ashoka's lion symbol appears on flags and coins, including the rupee. India was one of the first countries in the world to issue coins.

important educational institutions, similar to modern universities, were at Taxila, Ujjain and Varanasi.

Industry and Trade

Students who had to learn crafts and technical skills were trained not in monasteries but by the guilds that regulated various industries. The most important industries included textiles, mining, metalworking, jewellery-making and shipbuilding. The government provided facilities such as warehouses to encourage sea trade with foreign countries. It regulated weights and measures, provided guards for merchants on land and built new roads such as the Grand Trunk road between Pataliputra and Taxila.

Farming

In order to increase the amount of land under cultivation, the Mauryans oversaw the clearance of forests and encouraged people to move to the new regions. The chief crops included grains such as wheat, sesame, peppers, other vegetables, fruit and sugar cane. Farmers paid a tax in exchange for being able to farm on land that belonged to the empire. They paid a tax on the crops they produced and the animals they raised. They also paid a tax on water, which was supplied to the land by irrigation systems built by the empire.

The government employed a huge civil service to collect taxes. The taxes were used to support the royal family and to

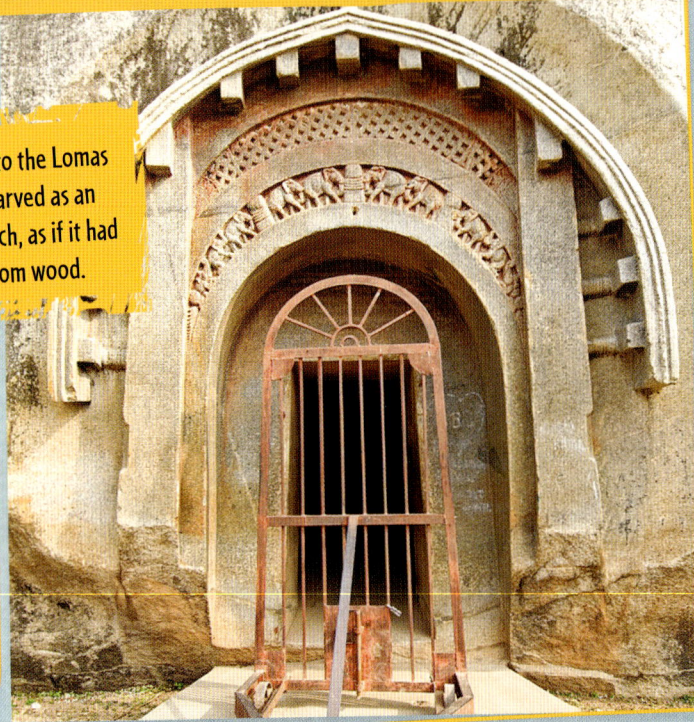

The entrance to the Lomas Rishi cave is carved as an elaborate porch, as if it had been made from wood.

Lomas Rishi Cave

One of Ashoka's public acts of religious devotion was to order the building of a series of chambers where Buddhist monks could retreat at the end of their wanderings. The most splendid was the Lomas Rishi cave. It was carved into a rock face to resemble a wooden building. There was even a carved thatched roof inside the cave. The walls had pillars like a wooden building – even though no pillars were needed to hold up the rock.

pay for public officials. With the revenue he raised, Ashoka also paid for many public projects to improve the lives of his subjects. He built waterways, canals, roads and rest houses for travellers. One of Ashoka's edicts told people how he had arranged medical help for his subjects.

During Ashoka's reign, the Mauryan Empire was characterised by peace. The principle of non-violence also extended to the treatment of animals. Ashoka stopped animal sacrifice and limited both hunting and fishing. In the 20th century, the Indian leader Mahatma Gandhi adopted a similar principle of non-violence when he led the campaign for Indian independence from Britain.

"All Men Are My Children"

Ashoka took his responsibilities as emperor seriously. He constantly travelled to see what was happening in the empire. He consulted his ministers often, but made all decisions about the empire himself. He employed advisers to check that the principles of *dhamma* (see pages 26–27) were being observed by his subjects.

Ashoka's construction programme relied on slave labour to build roads and other projects. However, he ordered that the

DAILY LIFE

The Untouchables

Although Ashoka did not try to change the caste system that shaped Indian society, he did try to ensure that all castes were treated fairly. This applied particularly to the lowest caste, the Sudras. The Sudras contained a smaller group known as the 'Untouchables'. They did jobs like disposing of dead bodies and getting rid of human waste. Other Hindus saw these jobs as unclean.

The Lomas Rishi cave is part of a group of of four Buddhist monuments that stands in the Barabar Hills in Bihar in India.

Life of the Buddha

Buddhism is based on the teachings of Siddhartha Gautama. Siddartha was born in present-day Nepal in 563 BCE. He was from a wealthy royal family. Aged 29, Siddartha realised that money would not bring him happiness. He spent six years studying and meditating until he reached a state known as 'Enlightenment'. He spent the rest of his life teaching *dhamma*, or truth, until his death. His teachings spread beyond India to the rest of the world.

slaves should be treated fairly. Slaves were also used in the empire's mines. Often, slaves came from one of the conquered kingdoms. They were given to the emperor as part of the payment of taxes. Slaves came from the lowest caste, the Sudras. They could buy their freedom, but they could never change their caste.

Expansion of Buddhism

Ashoka was responsible for the expansion of Buddhism across the Mauryan Empire and beyond its borders. He built up to 84,000 Buddhist monuments, called stupas. He also ordered the construction of Buddhist schools and monasteries and the publication of Buddhist texts.

The Great Stupa at Sanchi was built by Ashoka. Buddhists walked around dome-shaped stupas as an aid to meditation.

Buddha was said to have found Enlightenment while sitting under the Bodhi Tree in Bodh Gaya, India.

Ashoka maintained friendly relations with other Asian states. He is thought to have spread Buddhism to Afghanistan, Thailand and parts of North Asia, such as Siberia. One way Buddhism spread was through trade. Mauryan merchants who had converted to Buddhism took its religious message on their travels.

A Peaceful Empire

Ashoka ruled for 40 years. For over 30 of those – after the war with Kalinga – the empire was stable. There were no wars, and Ashoka did not invade other kingdoms. Historical accounts suggest that he did not disband the Mauryan army, however. The emperor knew that not all his neighbours or his subjects followed the same principle of non-violence.

DAILY LIFE

Spies!

As advised by Kautilya, the Mauryan emperors used a network of spies to keep control of the empire. The spies travelled widely. They gathered news of any threats or uprisings. They sent reports to government officials in Pataliputra. The fear of being reported by a spy helped maintain order even among those who were discontent with Mauryan rule.

Fall of the Empire

The strengths that made the Mauryan Empire the largest empire in the world under Ashoka would prove to be its undoing after his death, when a series of weak successors came to the throne.

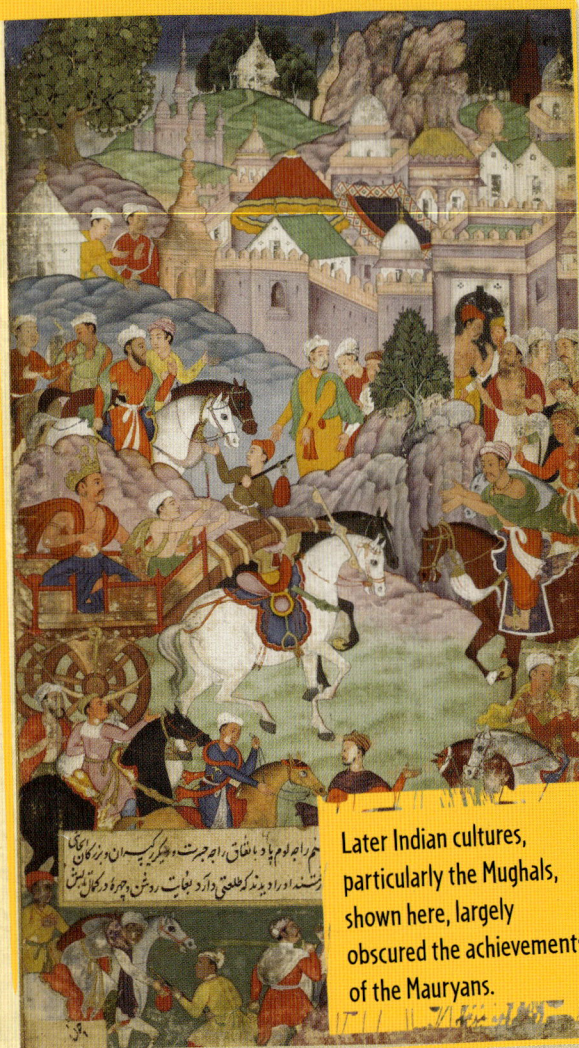

Later Indian cultures, particularly the Mughals, shown here, largely obscured the achievements of the Mauryans.

Ashoka died in 232 BCE. He left behind a vast empire ruled from Pataliputra. Although it appeared strong, the empire already showed signs of weakness.

One problem was the size of the empire. It was almost impossible to have efficient communications between Pataliputra and the small towns and villages that made up most of the empire. The kingdoms of the empire had little in common apart from being ruled by the Maurya. The people even spoke different languages. There was no sense of belonging or unity in the empire. In addition, the use of spies by the new Mauryan emperors caused great resentment. People did not feel any bond of trust with the emperor.

Even during the reign of Ashoka, some remote kingdoms had tried to break away from imperial rule. One cause of tension was the heavy tax burden imposed from Pataliputra. Under Ashoka, people accepted high taxes because the emperor carried out many

The burden of taxation on farmers and other subjects throughout the empire caused great resentment.

public works. Under the rulers who followed him, there was little sign of taxes being put to good use. More kingdoms began to think of rebellion.

A Weakened Empire

The weak emperors who followed Ashoka also faced pressure from their own nobles, the Brahman caste. The Brahmans had accepted Ashoka's conversion to Buddhism because in India the emperor had absolute control. They did not accept that his Buddhist principles were correct, however. After Ashoka's death, the Brahmans were eager to put pressure on the new emperor to return to the age-old teachings of Hinduism.

Mauryan Coins

The decline of the Mauryan Empire can be traced in its coins. All Mauryan rulers issued coins. The later coins, however, were of poor quality. They were punched out of metal rather than cast in a mould like earlier coins. Also unlike earlier coins, they were not made from pure silver. As taxes fell, the empire could no longer afford silver coins, so the silver was mixed with cheaper metals.

KEY PEOPLE

The Sunga

The Sunga dynasty ruled from Pataliputra after the fall of the Mauryan Empire. It took its name from General Pushyamitra Sunga. He assassinated the last Mauryan emperor, Brihadrata, in 185 BCE. Sunga took the throne and was the first of 10 Sunga rulers between 185 and 78 BCE. Warfare became frequent and Buddhism declined.

Some of the Brahmans argued that Ashoka's principle of non-violence had weakened the empire. The Mauryan Empire had, after all, been built on conquest. Without Ashoka's strong personality to hold the empire together, its internal kingdoms threatened to revolt and its neighbours drew up plans to invade.

The Last Emperor

In 185 BCE, less than fifty years after Ashoka's death, the Mauryan Empire came to an end. The last emperor, Brihadrata, was assassinated during a military parade by the Brahman general Pushyamitra

The Indo-Greeks

After the death of Brihadrata, the north-western empire came under the control of the Indo-Greeks. Demetrius, the Greco-Bactrian king, formed the new empire in around 180 BCE. The kingdom flourished for about a century before going into decline. The kingdom brought together Indian and Greek culture to create a unique blend of art and architecture. The Indo-Greeks also combined Buddhism with Greek religion, and were famed for their tolerant attitude.

Sunga. Sunga set up the Sunga dynasty, which would rule from Pataliputra for another century. There may also have been a rise in the power of Hinduism. Some ancient sources say that Buddhists were the victims of **persecution**.

The Sungas ruled only a small part of the former empire. In north-west India, the fall of the Mauryans left a **power vacuum**. In 180 BCE, the king of Bactria, Demetrius, invaded through the Khyber Pass. He created the Indo-Greek Kingdom in north-western India and southern Afghanistan. The Indo-Greek Kingdom lasted for about a century and was a centre of Buddhism. Although the ideas that had inspired Ashoka continued, the Mauryan Empire had disappeared forever.

This wall carving shows members of the Sunga royal family who ruled north-east India in the 2nd century BCE.

43

Timeline

c. 370 BCE	Birth of Kautilya, who will become the adviser to the Mauryan emperors.
c. 340 BCE	Birth of Chandragupta Maurya.
326 BCE	Alexander the Great reaches the borders of Gandhara, but his army forces him to turn back.
322 BCE	Chandragupta comes to the throne after defeating the Nanda dynasty of Magadha.
319–317 BCE	Changdraupta defeats kingdoms in north-western India to establish an empire.
303 BCE	Chandragupta agrees a treaty with the Bactrian ruler Seleucus I Nicator to fix the north-western border of the empire in return for 500 war elephants.
c. 290s BCE	The Greek diplomat Megasthenes describes the Mauryan Empire in his book *Indica*.
298 BCE	Chandragupta gives up the throne to pursue the Jain religion. His son, Bindusara, becomes emperor.
272 BCE	Bindusara dies.
c. 268 BCE	Having murdered his half-brother Susima, Ashoka comes to the throne.

c. 260 BCE   Ashoka goes to war against Kalinga, which he brings into the empire. The bloodshed and loss of life convince him to turn to Buddhism.

c. 250 BCE   Ashoka begins building Buddhist stupas and other monuments.

232 BCE   The death of Ashoka marks the beginning of the decline of the Mauryan Empire. He is succeeded by Dasaratha.

224 BCE   Dasaratha is succeeded by Emperor Samprati.

215 BCE   Salisuka comes to the throne.

202 BCE   Devavarman becomes emperor.

195 BCE   Satadhanvan succeeds Devavarman.

187 BCE   Devavarman is replaced by the last emperor, Brihadrata.

185 BCE   The last Mauryan emperor, Brihadrata, is assassinated during a military parade by the chief of his guard, General Pushyamitra Sunga, who establishes the Sunga dynasty.

180 BCE   Bactrian Greeks led by Demetrius invade through the Khyber Pass and establish the new Indo-Greek Kingdom.

78 BCE   The Sunga dynasty is overthrown.

Glossary

alms Money or food given to monks or to the poor.

assassinate To murder someone for a political reason.

caste One of the four traditional classes into which all Hindus were born.

centralised Describes a state where political power is concentrated in the capital.

convert To change from one religious belief to another.

diplomat An official who represents his or her country abroad.

dynasty A series of rulers who are members of the same family.

edict An official announcement made by someone in authority.

Hindi A widely spoken language in northern India.

illiterate Unable to read or write.

immunity Being protected from disease or being excused from taxes.

imperial Related to an empire.

karma The idea that a person's actions in one life influence their fate in future lives.

missionaries People sent on a mission to promote a religion.

novice A person who is being trained to join a religious order.

nomads People who travel from place to place and have no permanent home.

non-violence The use of peaceful means for political or social change.

persecution Hostility towards and ill-treatment of a group of people because of their race or religion.

power vacuum A situation in which a region has no central government or authority.

reincarnation The rebirth of a soul in a new body after death.

stupa A dome-shaped building that is used as a shrine by Buddhists.

subcontinent The peninsula of South Asia that contains the modern countries of India, Pakistan and Bangladesh.

tolerance A willingness to put up with opinions or behaviour that one disagrees with.

treatise A written work that deals with a subject in a thorough way.

Further Reading

Books

Brooks, Susie, *India* (Unpacked), Wayland, 2014.

Chopra, Sunny, *India* (The Real), Franklin Watts, 2014.

Gill, David, *Alexander the Great* (People Who Made History), Franklin Watts, 2016.

Head, Honor, *Buddhism* (Our Places of Worship), Wayland, 2009.

Steele, Philip, *Empires* (Epic!), Wayland, 2015.

Teece, Geoff, *Hinduism* (Religion in Focus), Franklin Watts, 2008.

Websites

Ancient India – The British Museum
www.ancientindia.co.uk
Explore the people, culture, beliefs and history of ancient India using animations, 3D models and objects from the British Museum's collections.

BBC History – Ancient India
www.bbc.co.uk/history/ancient/india
An exploration of the ancient sites that helped to shape the history and culture of Pakistan and northern India (archived site).

Timemap of World History
www.timemaps.com/civilization-the-mauryan-empire
A guide to the society, religions and major figures of the Mauryan Empire.

Index